ABC with *Bernadette Thérèse*

MAT DE SOUSA

Aa
is for Angel

... who guards me as I play

Bb
is for Blessings

... which brighten up my day

Dd
is for Deacon

... who reads the Word of the Lord

Ee
is for Easter

... when God changed our fate

Ff
is for Fish

... what Jesus and his friends ate

Gg
is for Grapes

... which are turned into wine

Ii
is for Icon

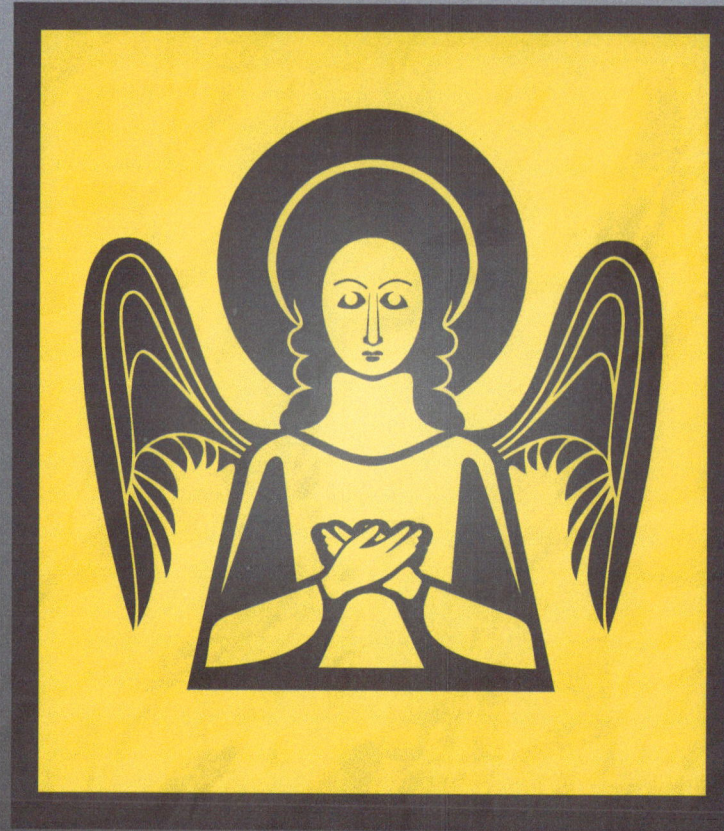

... an image beautiful to see

Ll
is for Lamp

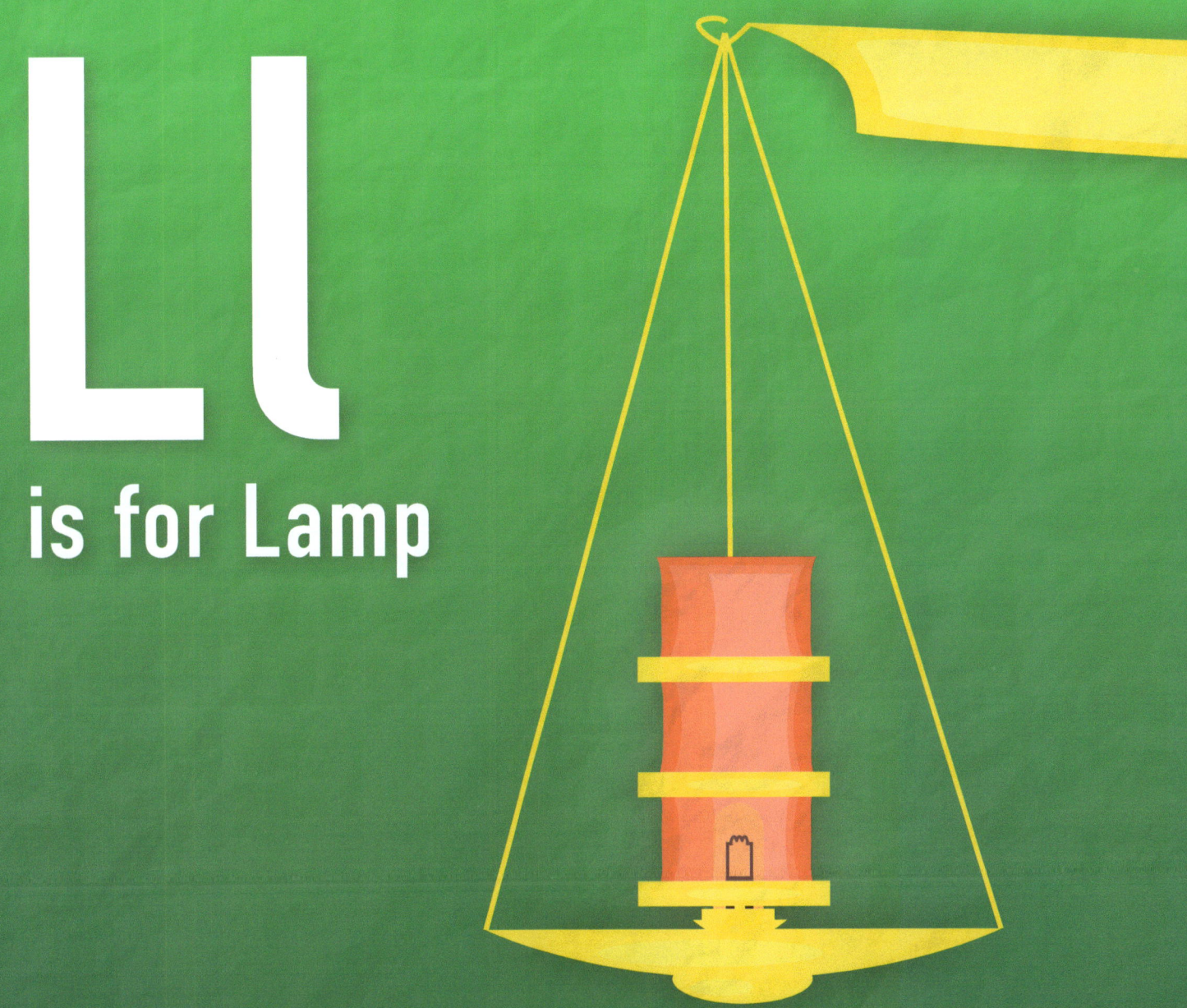

... which tells us Jesus is inside

Mm
is for Mary

... who cares for me as her child

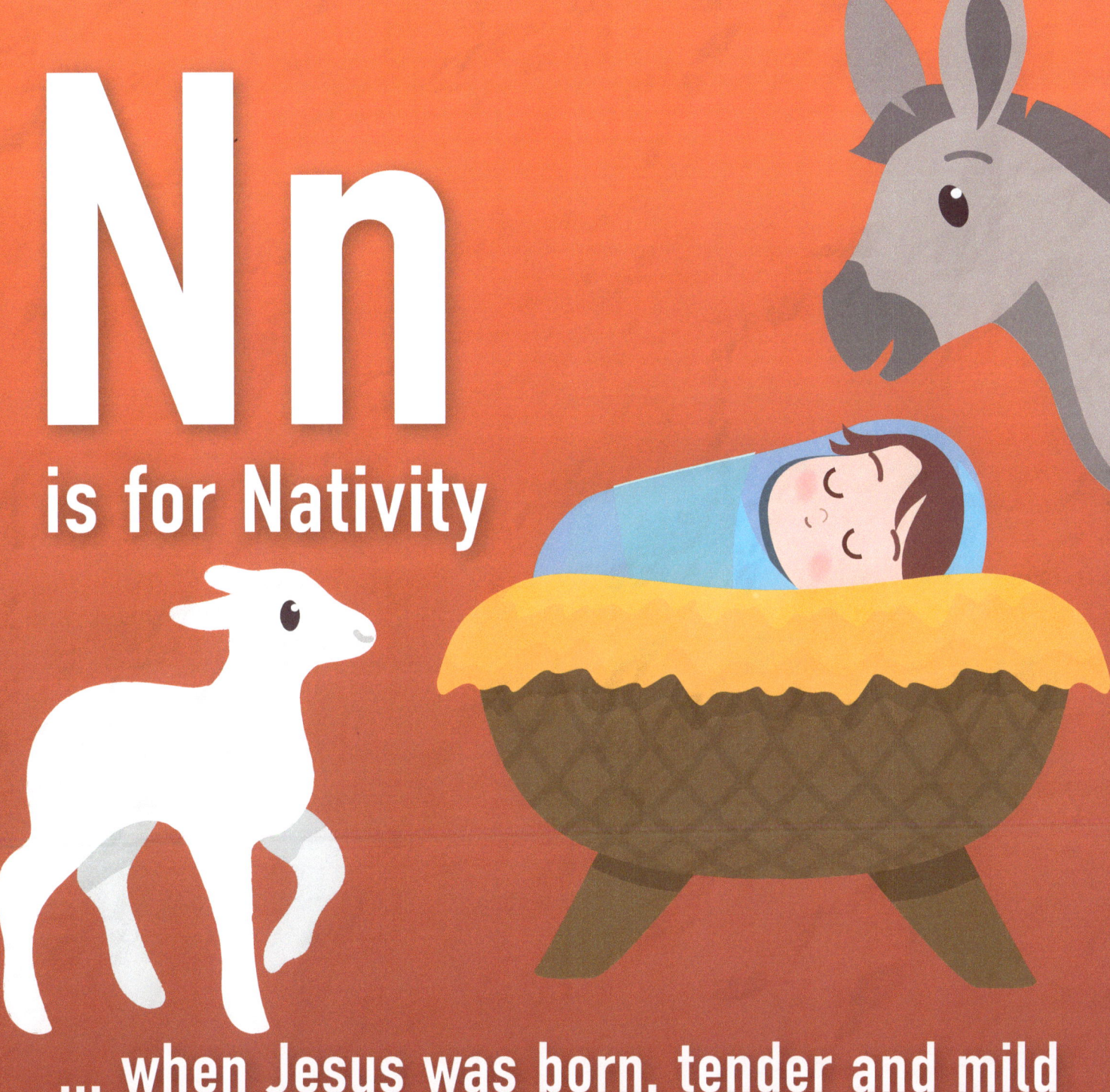

Pp
is for Prayer

... how God and I speak

Qq
is for Queen

... Mary's title that we say

Rr
is for Rosary

... the beads we use to pray

Ss
is for Saint

... who helps us from the heavens

Tt
is for Teaching

... Jesus' important lessons

Uu
is for Unity

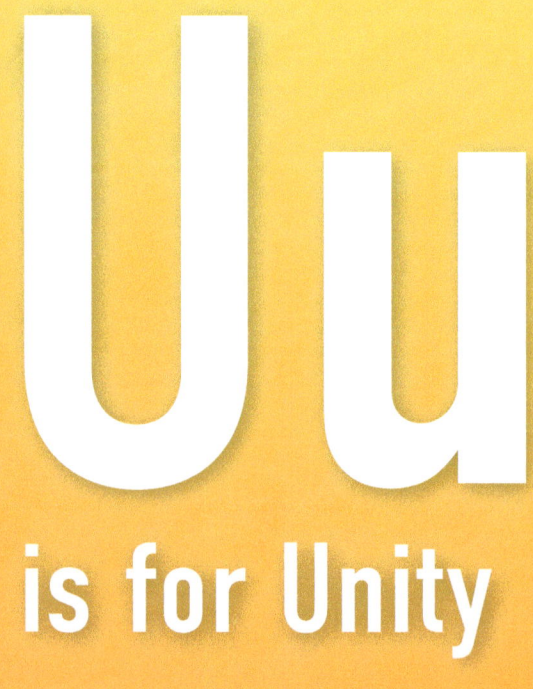

... when we all work together

Vv
is for Victory

... Jesus has won forever!

Ww
is for Worship

... how we thank the Lord above

Xx
stands for Cross

... the greatest act of love

Yy
is for Yes

... which set God's plan in motion

Zz
is for Zeal

... when we share our devotion

www.ingramcontent.com/pod-product-compliance
Lightning Source LLC
Chambersburg PA
CBHW040731150426
42811CB00063B/1574